PLATO'S VIEW OF MAN

BY THE SAME AUTHOR

*A Dialogue between
Bergson, Aristotle, and Philologos*

*Man and the Universe
in American Philosophy*

*Modern Greek Philosophers
on the Human Soul*

Byzantine Thought and Art

Modern Greek Thought

Plato's Theory of Fine Art

PLATO'S VIEW OF MAN

Two Bowen Prize Essays dealing with the
Problem of the Destiny of Man and the
Individual Life, together with Selected Passages from Plato's Dialogues on Man and
the Human Soul.

BY

CONSTANTINE CAVARNOS

INSTITUTE FOR BYZANTINE
AND MODERN GREEK STUDIES
115 Gilbert Road
Belmont, Massachussetts
U.S.A.

CONTENTS

PREFACE

In this volume I have brought together two essays on Plato that I wrote at an early stage in my philosophical development, and an anthology of passages from Plato's dialogues which I recently compiled and translated from the original Greek texts. The first of these essays, *The Problem of the Destiny of Man*, is a product of a research course on Plato which I took under the direction of the late Professor Raphael Demos, when I was a graduate student in philosophy at Harvard University. It won the Francis Bowen Prize in 1945. The second essay, *The Individual Life*, is a product of a course on Plato's philosophy that was given by the late Professor John D. Wild. It was composed when I was a junior at Harvard and won the Bowen Prize in 1941. These essays were written as term papers for the respective courses, and were submitted in revised form for the Bowen Prize, which is conferred annually by Harvard University "for the best essay upon a subject in moral or political philosophy."

8

The essays appear now in print for the first time. In preparing them for publication, I have abridged them and made many revisions.

It is obviously impossible in two brief essays to discuss or even touch upon every aspect of Plato's teaching on man. In order to amplify somewhat this teaching, I have added a chapter of selected passages from various dialogues of Plato that bring to the attention of the reader other elements of Plato's view of man, or further clarify some of those dealt with in the two essays. These selections have the additional value of acquainting with Plato's style and mode of thought those readers who have not had occasion to read his works.

I owe many thanks to my former colleague Professor Holcombe M. Austin of Wheaton College (Mass.) for reading the first two chapters and suggesting a number of improvements.

January, 1975

THE PROBLEM OF THE DESTINY OF MAN*

1. Philosophic Wonder

Philosophy, says Plato in the *Theaetetus*, begins with wonder (*to thaumazein*). By wonder he does not mean wonder in general. For, as he points out in the *Republic*, "if mere curiosity makes a philosopher, you will find many a strange being will have a title to the name." [1] Philosophic wonder for Plato is ultimately wonder about *man* (*anthropos*). The philosopher "inquires and exerts himself to find out what a human being is and what is proper for such a nature to do or bear different from any other." [2]

Plato's fundamental problem is not an academic, but a real one. At the beginning of his philosophical vocation he raises a great question, the question about human existence—about

---

* Abridged and revised version of the 1945 Bowen Prize Essay, *The Problem of the Destiny of Man in Plato*.

the *whole* of human existence, and not merely about some particular phase of it. He is not concerned primarily with finding the principles underlying any one science, or group of sciences, or science in general; or with developing a system that will bring him fame; or with developing a method that will enable men to make discoveries which will give them power to control nature and ameliorate the material conditions of mankind. None of these philosophic orientations raises the question which distressed Plato and which he considered as the most fundamental, since the answer that is given to it will determine the kind of answer that will be given to questions connected with all the phases of human existence.

Francis Bacon started philosophizing because he was dissatisfied with the material lot of man and dreamed of bringing about the Kingdom of Man on Earth. Descartes started philosophizing not because he was dissatisfied with man's material lot, but because he was dissatisfied with the knowledge of his time and place, all of which, with the exception of mathematics, he found unclear and uncertain. His philosophic wonder sprang from this dissatisfaction. Plato's wonder, on the other hand, arose from a dissatisfaction that went far deeper, that affected the inmost depths of his being. And it was this that made Plato not simply a thinker, but a very ardent thinker. Plato started philosophizing not merely because he was dissatisfied with the material lot of man, or with the knowledge of his time, but because he was dissatisfied with the whole of man's earthly existence, considered from the cognitive, the aesthetic, the ethical, and the religious standpoint.

Both Plato and Descartes began with scepticism, both raised doubt not only about prevailing beliefs, but also about their own beliefs. But Plato's doubt was *felt, real,* whereas Descartes' doubt was largely only *pretended, academic.* Descartes started "doubting everything," as he tells us in his *Discourse on Method;* yet he went on living as though nothing had occurred in his inner world. His scepticism did not extend to theology, ethics, and politics. It touched only the surface of his being and hence did not alter his mode of living. Had there been any genuine scepticism, such as we find very clearly in Socrates, Plato, St. Augustine, Pascal and Kierkegaard, in the early stage of their spiritual development, the whole course of his life would have changed. But there was no thorough shaking-up of the deeper, subconscious level of the soul, such as would have brought to consciousness his deeply-held beliefs.

Plato's real doubt proceeded, I suggest, in some such way as follows: "I find myself on the earth, among other beings like myself. I observe that of these beings some die and are as if they had never been. It is plain that a similar fate awaits the rest of them and . . . myself. The life of these beings seems to consist in the brief period between birth and death. This ephemeral existence is one consisting largely of perpetual struggling, suffering, and need.[3] 'No human thing is of serious importance, and grief stands in the way of that which at the moment is most required.'[4] Human society is characterized by ignorance, triviality, cruelty, and injustice; it puts to death a man like Socrates, 'the wisest, most just, and best man.'[5] What is called history appears to be nothing but a meaningless cyclical affair, where states and civilizations rise, flourish, and decline.[6] Now is this all there is to human life? Is the individual 'but a walking shadow, a poor player that struts and frets his hour upon the stage, and then is heard no more?'[7] Is man—am *I*—merely an empirical and ephemeral phenomenon, here on earth for an insignificantly brief period of time, destined to annihilation at death? Or am I something more than the body that dies and disintegrates? Can it be that that in my body which thinks, wills, feels, and is conscious—the soul—is something other than the body and essentially independent of it, and hence capable of surviving the disintegration of the body? But again, supposing that the soul *is* something other than the body and independent of it and more enduring; still, is it not possible that the soul, 'after having worn out many bodies, might at last perish itself upon leaving its last body?' [8] However, it may be that the individual soul is immortal, indestructible. And there may be another, unseen realm of being, where a soul that has become duly purified and perfected may eternally behold perfect Truth, Goodness, and Beauty.

"These, for me, now that I have begun to reflect seriously, are the most important questions. They are questions that are terribly pressing and must be answered one way or the other. The answer I shall arrive at will determine how I am going to live, will determine what I shall do with myself. I shall continue my meditations; and if I become convinced of the first alternative, that I am merely an ephemeral phenomenon, I shall try to forget the fact of death, to erase it from my mind if possible, by engaging unceasingly in the distractions of everyday life. Or, I shall occupy myself with creating temporary and corruptible values that will help me forget death. Or, again, perhaps if I really become convinced of this view, I shall find that I will have to do away with myself; for the whole thing becomes irrational, meaningless: 'I live in the midst of a lie, and die for a lie, and the earth is a lie, and rests on a lie, on a stupid derision.' [9] If, on the other hand, I become convinced that this alternative is false, and that the other one is true, the complexion of the whole situation changes.

And I shall say to myself: I will live for immortality; I will pursue with all the ardor I can command the path that leads to a higher, supremely good, eternal level of being." [10]

2. Immortality

Plato became convinced that the second alternative was true. Now Descartes, having gone through his methodological doubt, proceeded to his first indubitable truth: "I think, therefore, I am." From this truth he went on to infer the existence of God and then the existence of the external, material world. Having done this, he devoted himself to the study of mathematics and physics, anatomy and physiology. Plato, on the other hand, who never doubted the existence of the external world and who would, I presume, have smiled at Descartes' "proofs" of its existence, having gone through the torturing experience of real doubt about the most vital issues, gradually proceeded to the conclusion that the soul is immortal and that there is a world imperceptible to sense, a realm of eternity to which the soul is destined.

The Greek philosopher might have stated his conclusion as follows: "After much doubt and prolonged reflection, I have become convinced that I am essentially an immortal being, whose true abode is a world of absolute truth, goodness, and beauty. But I know this only from certain convergent lines of facts, not with absolute certainty.[11] I must now endeavor to pass from vagueness to clarity, from probability to absolute knowledge. I must try to discover with the greatest clarity and certainty possible, all that I can about myself and the way in which I ought to arrange my life with a view to an immortal existence in the realm of true being."

3. Self-Knowledge

Superior *self-knowledge* becomes now the *main concern* of the philosopher. At this stage of his career, Plato sees that "the unexamined life is not worth living," [12] and that one should neglect all other studies and seek after this study, "by what means and by what modes of living we shall best navigate our barque of life through this voyage of existence." [13] In the *Gorgias* he has Socrates say: "I consider how I may be able to show my judge [in Hades] that my soul is in the best health. So giving the go-by to the honors that most men seek, I shall try, by inquiry into the truth, to be really good in as high a degree as I am able, both in my life and, when I come to die, in my death. And I invite all other men likewise, to the best of my power . . . to this contest, which I say is worth all other contests on this earth." [14] The main concern of Plato is to acquire knowledge—in the stricter sense of the term—about the nature of man, and from this

to deduce the *final object* of all of man's toils:
his *supreme good* and the *necessary means* for
attaining it. For if we know the nature of man,
"we are likely to know what pains to take over
ourselves; but if we do not, we never can." [15]

Now to attain genuine knowledge about the
nature of man is a most difficult task. It was
no mere scamp who inscribed the words "Know
thyself" on the temple at Delphi.[16] For it
is impossible fully to discern the nature of the
soul, unless one has studied and learned what
is true and what is false of the *whole of existence.*
The knowledge that is needed of man is not
of man as an isolated being, as an abstraction,
but as an integral being, in all his aspects and
in all his significant relations to reality as a
whole. Thus, to treat of man the philosopher
must treat of the whole of reality. He must acquire a knowledge and understanding of the
whole universe.[17]

4. Cosmology and Theology

At this point anthropology, or theory of man,
passes into cosmology, or theory of the cosmos,
and theology, or theory of God. This is noticeable
in Plato's later dialogues: the *Republic, Symposium, Phaedrus, Statesman, Laws* and so on,
and in his *Epistles.* In his early, so-called "So-
cratic," dialogues, man is not envisaged in this
broad context. Further, in his early writings
there is frequently an expression of doubt, un-

certainty, hesitation. Most of the dialectical discussions leave the problem with which they start unsolved. In the later dialogues, on the other hand, Plato generally adopts an expository instead of an argumentative style, and a more positive and confident attitude. He presents a fairly comprehensive teaching about man and the universe, and speaks as one who is in possession not of mere conjectures, but of real knowledge about man and the cosmos, and who realizes the inadequacy of language as a medium of expressing it.[18]

How did Plato acquire this knowledge, which was not provided by his master Socrates? Was it the result of his own insights, or was it obtained from others during his travels in Greece, Southern Italy—where he visited the Pythagoreans—and Egypt? Of both, it seems. In his works there are references to non-Greek cultures, including expressions of high esteem for them.[19] It seems that Plato did gather much important knowledge during his travels abroad, but what he gathered in this way he assimilated, made his own. In the *Epinomis*, which was composed by his pupil and secretary Philip as a supplement to the *Laws*, we find this significant statement: "Whatever the Greeks acquire from foreigners is finally turned by them into something nobler." [20] And in the *Seventh Epistle*, Plato seems to be speaking from personal experience when he says that the knowledge of "the highest and first truths of nature" is "brought to birth in the soul on a sudden, as light that is kindled by a leaping spark and thereafter nourishes itself." [21]

The knowledge to which I am referring is expressible—though inadequately—by statements such as the following: The world is a totality of things ordered by mathematical, aesthetic, and moral laws.[22] The ultimate ground of the world is a Being—God—that is both immanent in the world and transcendent of it.[23] God is its Maker, Ruler, Father and Judge,[24] and is absolutely good and the cause only of what is good, never of what is evil.[25] God orders all things "with a view to the preservation and excellence of the Whole, whereof each part, so far as it can, does and suffers what is proper to it. To each of these parts, down to the smallest fraction, rulers of their action and passion are appointed to bring about fulfillment even to the uttermost fraction." [26] All created things may be dissolved by God's will, which is mightiest and most sovereign, but God will not dissolve that which is beautifully joined together and sound, for that would be the deed of a wicked one.[27] The divine Judge shifts "the character that grows better to a superior place, and the worse to a worse place, according to what best suits each of them, so that each may be allowed its appropriate destiny." [28] Man has a divine origin and destiny. He is a celestial and not an earthly creature, being potentially a likeness of God.[29] A man's fate after death, the degree of immortality that he will achieve, is determined by his way of life on earth: "Whoso indulges in lusts or in contentions and devotes himself overmuch thereto must of necessity be filled with opinions that are wholly mortal and altogether, so far as it is possible to become mortal, fall not short of this in even a small degree, inasmuch as he has made great his mortal part. But he who has seriously devoted himself to learning and to true thoughts, and has exercised these qualities above all others, must necessarily and inevitably think thoughts that are immortal and divine, if he lays hold on truth, and in so far as it is possible for human nature to partake of immortality, he must fall short thereof in no degree." [30]

5. Ethics

Plato's ethics, his teaching regarding man's ultimate purpose in life and the necessary means for attaining it, is closely connected with these important ideas. If man is to attain salvation, he must strive to become as far as possible like God. Salvation, the attainment of a higher level of being, the achievement of true immortality, can come only through such striving. "We ought," says the Athenian philosopher, "to try to flee from earth to the dwelling of the gods as quickly as we can; and to 'flee' is to become like God, as far as this is possible." [31] Again, he remarks: "Every man ought to make up his mind that he will be one of the followers of God." [32]

Now God is Mind, Intelligence, Reason. Therefore, man ought to live, as far as possible, a life which involves the constant use of reason, and which conforms to the dictates of reason. We must say: "and which conforms to the dictates of reason," because man is not wholly intelligence or reason, but has in him a non-rational part that is in need of enlightenment and control, that must be fashioned in the image of the rational. God is perfectly rational, perfectly orderly. Hence man—since his goal is to become as much as possible like God—ought to strive to become himself perfectly orderly. Just as God, the supreme Maker or Artist (*Demiourgos*), brings order into chaos and produces the orderly world, so man ought to strive to introduce order and harmony into his own body and soul, transforming himself from a micro-chaos into a microcosmos.

For Plato the study of mathematics becomes not merely an indispensable intellectual discipline for the philosopher, but also a practice of imitating God. "A man," he says, "cannot fail to imitate that with which he holds converse with wonder and delight." [33] Now the objects of geometry—the straight line and the circle and the plane and solid figures that are formed from these—possess measure and proportion, and therefore beauty, "since measure and proportion are everywhere identified with beauty." [34] Therefore, in contemplating the objects or geometry "with wonder and delight," man himself acquires measure and proportion, or inner, super-sensible beauty, which is possessed eminently by God.

The contemplation of the fixed, mathematically expressible motions of the heavenly bodies and that of the immaterial, unchanging, eternal, divine archetypes or ideas has the same valuable effect upon us. The lover or wisdom, the man who is striving for self-perfection, therefore studies "the harmonies and revolutions of the universe," [35] and explores dialectically the realm of eternal ideas. He contemplates things that "abide in harmony, as reason bids; and these he endeavors to imitate and, as far as he can, to fashion himself in their likeness and assimilate himself to them . . . Associating with divine order, he will himself become orderly and divine in the measure permitted to man." [36]

Also important for ordering and transforming man is the philosophical method of investigation known as the *elenchos*—the process of examining one's beliefs, opinions, and feelings. Man suffers from inner deformity or ugliness, from disease of the psyche. He is a deformed being in need of harmony, of beauty; he is a sick being, in need of therapy. Now his deformity and disease consist of two kinds of ignorance: conscious ignorance (*agnoia*) and unconscious ignorance (*amathia*), and of cowardice, intemperance and injustice.[37] The last three vices are manifestations of inner discord, of insubordination of the lower to the higher faculties; and in the worst cases, of the subservience of the highest to the lowest faculty. Their cause is ignorance. Our efforts, therefore, should be directed towards getting rid of our ignorance.

We have noted that there are two kinds of ignorance—conscious and unconscious. Conscious ignorance is ignorance of which a person is cognizant. Thus, if one does not know what holiness is and recognizes the fact that he does not know, he is said to be in a state of conscious ignorance as regards this virtue. But if one does not know what holiness is, yet thinks he knows, then he is in a state of *un*conscious ignorance regarding holiness. Plato gives vivid expression to such ignorance in the person of Euthyphro in the dialogue by this name. Unconscious ignorance is far worse than conscious ignorance. The latter may become the starting point of the pursuit of knowledge and of inner development, whereas unconscious ignorance prevents one from seeking knowledge and growing within, inasmuch as the unconsciously ignorant man believes himself to be already in possession of knowledge, and imagines himself to be a much better person than he really is.[38] Unconscious ignorance assumes the form of pride, conceit, prejudice, and leads to contentious and false sophistry.[39] Now the *elenchos* is "the greatest and most efficacious method of purification" (*katharsis*) from this ignorance.[40] It purifies "the soul from conceits that stand in the way of knowledge." [41] The proper use of this method results in intellectual integrity and inner health. It brings about a harmony between what a person thinks he knows and what he really knows, between what he professes to believe and what he really believes, between what he pretends to doubt and what he really doubts, between what he imagines himself to be and what he really is.

By contemplating objects that possess or observe measure and proportion—the objects of mathematics, the heavenly bodies, and the eternal archetypes or ideas—and by purifying himself through the practice of self-examination, the lover of wisdom becomes more and more orderly and harmonious, more and more Godlike. His whole soul becomes converted from darkness to light, from untruth to truth, from the changing to the unchanging, from becoming to being, from disunity to unity. His inner vision becomes increasingly clear and steady and able to contemplate the Being that is "the starting point of all," [42] that "sheds light on all," [43] that is "the cause of knowledge and truth," [44] that is supremely real, good, and beautiful.[45] Having risen to this level, "he is destined to win the friendship of God; he above all men is immortal." [46]

The practice of imitating God does not stop here. God, according to Plato, is not only transcendent of the world of creatures, but is also immanent in it. God is not only "thought thinking itself," as Aristotle later was to say; He not only "abides in His own proper and wonted state," [47] but is also will and providence active in the world. Hence, if man is to be complete in his imitation of God, if he is to attain his full stature, he must also concern himself with his fellow men and strive to enlighten and regenerate them, too, as far as this is possible.[48] Having ascended to the world of light, knowledge and perfection, one must descend periodically to the world of darkness, ignorance and imperfection, where the vast majority of men live, and through his knowledge and understanding help them move upward.

THE INDIVIDUAL LIFE*

1. Immortality of the Human Soul

"Neither man nor nation can live without a 'higher idea,' and there is only one such idea on this earth, that of an immortal human soul; all other 'higher ideas' by which men live flow from that. . . . Following the loss of the idea of immortality, suicide appears a complete and ineluctable necessity for every man who is in the slightest degree above the level of the beasts of the field. . . . The idea of immortality is life itself, the definitive formulation and first source of the truth and integrity of conscience." So thought the author of *The Diary of a Writer*, a man who, although commonly known only as a novelist, was also a profound philosopher: Feodor Dostoievsky.[1] In a like vein, Vladimir

---

* Abridged and revised version of the 1941 Bowen Prize Essay, *Plato and the Individual Life: An Interpretation of Plato's Conception of the Individual Life, with Special Reference to Christian Thought and Modern Philosophy.*

Solovyev says: "Two associated aspirations, like two invisible wings, raise the human soul above the rest of created nature: the hunger for *immortality* and the thirst for *truth* or moral perfection. Either without the other is meaningless. . . . Endless life without truth and perfection would be an eternity of torment, and perfection without immortality would be rank injustice and indignity without measure.[2]

Such was the belief of Plato also. The idea of an immortal human soul is central in his philosophy and is specially dealt with in his *Apology, Phaedo, Phaedrus, Republic, Symposium, Timaeus, Laws*, and other dialogues.

Plato gives ten main arguments for the immortality of the soul. They are, briefly, the following:

(i) *The instinctive aspiration after immortality testifies to the immortality of the soul.* This argument appears in the *Symposium*,[3] where Plato discusses the nature of *eros*, in the *Laws*, and elsewhere. In the *Laws* he exhorts: "As far as the principle of immortality dwells in us, to that we must hearken, both in public and private life."[4] Emerson,[5] Fiske,[6] Bergson and others have held a similar view. "When a strong instinct assures the probability of personal survival," says Bergson, "men have the right not to close their ears to its voice."[7]

(ii) *Since vice, which is the peculiar disease*

_of the soul, does not destroy but at most deforms
it, the soul must be indestructible._[8] But it may
be argued that moral disease may completely
disrupt the unity of personality, so that an individual may come to have in himself nothing
personal but what is mortal. Plato recognizes
this; but still for him this would not be equivalent
to annihilation: an impersonal ego would still
survive. Similarly, the Christian believes in the
immortality of *all* human souls, although he
views only the souls of the virtuous as being
spiritually alive, and regards those of the wicked
as being spiritually dead even during the present, earthly life.

(iii) *It is reasonable to suppose, by analogy,
that since the processes of nature are in general
cyclical—e.g. night passes into day and day into
night, winter passes into summer and summer
into winter, and so on—life also is cyclical:
the dead return to life, just as the living die;
and that the soul is therefore immortal. Were
this not the case, life would ultimately vanish
from the universe.*[9] This argument implies the
destruction of the personality sometime after
the death of the body, and hence carries no
weight for the Christian, for whom personality
is the highest value. Interestingly, Plato himself
asserts in another connection that the philosopher who has achieved a high degree of inner
perfection escapes from the "wheel of rebirth."
After death his soul will dwell forever with

the gods as a pure spirit. Plato evidently asserts the indestructibility of personality in such cases.[10]

(iv) *Knowledge involves universals, sense presents only particulars; hence, knowledge precedes sensation. This implies the existence of the soul prior to the body: sense-experience merely enables the soul to recall the universals or eternal ideas which it contemplated when it lived in a disembodied state.*[11] Plato directs this argument against the epiphenomenalists, who say that the soul is merely a by-product of the body, just as a harmony is a by-product of a musical instrument, and perishes along with the body at death. Now if the soul existed prior to the body, it cannot be a by-product of the body, but must be essentially independent of the body and should survive the death of the body.

The argument does not necessarily imply *impersonal immortality, unless we view the soul as a *static* entity. However, the soul is *not* static, but *dynamic*; and the achievement of personality—of an integrated, ethical, self-conscious ego with memory—involves the differentiation of a premordial and undifferentiated ego. Personality once achieved is not only retained but may go on growing. It should be added that one may accept the thesis that we have innate knowledge of universals without accepting the theory of preexistence. Such knowledge may be accounted for in other ways.

(v) *The soul is simple, uncompounded, and what is uncompounded cannot disintegrate.*[12] But at other times Plato speaks of the soul as something far from simple, as consisting of various faculties or powers. It does not follow that he is involved in a contradiction; for as Bergson points out, *both unity and multiplicity are given* in the experience of our personality or self, and to assert the reality of one is not to deny the reality of the other.[13]

(vi) *The soul is closely akin to the divine, archetypal ideas, these being apprehended only by thought, and both the ideas and thought being invisible, non-sensible. Now as the ideas are incorruptible, eternal, it is probable that the soul, too, is incorruptible and deathless.*[14] In many of his dialogues Plato asserts and seeks to prove that besides the realm of visible, material things, there is a realm of invisible, immaterial things, which embraces the ideas and man's higher faculties. The fact that we are capable of apprehending eternal ideas or universals, which are immaterial and incorruptible, is taken to imply that there is in us something immaterial and indestructible. When we die, it is the body, which belongs to the realm of visible and destructible things, that dies. The part of ourselves which belongs to the invisible realm—our soul—survives.

(vii) *The soul participates essentially in the idea of life and excludes the opposite of life, death.*[15] This argument hinges on Plato's theory of "participation" (*methexis*). That some such view is involved in the Christian conception of immortality is undeniable. But the "life" in which the soul participates is not for the Christian an abstract idea, but the grace of the Holy Spirit. Only in so far as a man comes to partake of this does he become truly alive and immortal. And conversely, to the extent that a man alienates himself from God he becomes dead. But the limit of complete death of a soul is never reached.

(viii) *The soul is a "self-moving" principle; its motion—described by the terms will, consideration, attention, deliberation, opinion, joy and sorrow, confidence, fear, hatred, love—consequently its life, is therefore perpetual, unending.*[16] This argument brings in the concept of dynamism, which I remarked is necessary for the fourth argument.

(ix) *The superior dignity and value of the soul argue for its survival of the crass human body.*[17] This argument, with various modifications, seems to be the proof most commonly adopted by modern philosophers to support the belief in immortality. It has been used, for instance, by Kant,[18] Lotze,[19] and Münsterberg.[20] The proof assumes that the universe is *moral* and consequently value cannot perish. Such an argument does not promise immortality to all: it is the immort*ability* rather than the immor*tality* of the soul that it affirms. Thus,

Plato remarks that "God will not dissolve that which is beautifully joined together and sound, for that would be the deed of a wicked one." [21] And Lotze says: "We hold the principle to be valid, that everything which has once originated will endure forever, as soon as it possesses an unalterable value for the coherent system of the world; but it will, as a matter of course, in turn cease to be, if this is not the case." [22]

(x) *The world demands a future existence for the rectification of the injustices of this life.*[23] "If death were the end of all, the wicked would have had a bargain in dying, for they would have been happily quit not only of their body, but of their own evil together with their souls;" [24] and the virtuous would have had no recompense after the present life.[25]

Like the preceding argument, this assumes that the universe is moral, just.

2. Structure of the Soul

In the myth of the *Phaedrus*,[26] the human soul is compared to a chariot drawn by two winged horses, one noble and the other ignoble, and guided by a pilot. The noble horse represents the "spirited" or honor-and-power-seeking part of the psyche, while the ignoble one represents the "appetitive" part, the animal desires. The pilot represents *noesis*, the purely cognitive aspect of reason. In the case of the developed, genuinely philosophical psyche, the horses have

wings full of feathers, so that the chariot
can move not only forward but also upward,
to the realm of perfect being. These wings
represent the emotional side of reason, which
Plato calls *eros*, love. The wings are related
to the whole vehicle, but more closely to the
pilot, for if he is a bad leader the wings will
be smashed. The horses can pull the chariot
forward, but it is the pilot that has to guide
them *upward*. Each horse has an independent
power of his own, but the noble steed *obeys*
the charioteer, while the ignoble one *dis*obeys
him. In the healthy soul, the pilot—the cognitive
aspect of reason—is master, and the ignoble
steed—the desiring part of the soul—has been
transformed and is fully obedient.

Plato does not separate reason from emotion,
as we are apt to do today. For him, as Professor
Raphael Demos points out, "reason is not merely detached understanding: it is conviction fired
with enthusiasm. The highest rapture possible
to man is the rapture of the contemplation of
the ideas. The pursuit of knowledge is animated
by the eros for the ideas; and the final truth
cannot be conveyed by concepts. So Plato has
recourse to myths and allegories and vivid, un-
forgettable images, in order to convey the ultimate truths." [27]

The pursuit of knowledge by the soul is repre-
sented allegorically by the soul's journey
through the heavens. The charioteer with dif-

ficulty drives the horses; he has to struggle constantly with the wild sensuality of the ignoble steed; and while listening to the call of eros, to rational aspiration, he directs the desires and flight forward and upward towards the highest celestial realm, where the gods dwell and pursue their course, happy in their beatific vision. "Colorless, formless, intangible Being is visible only to reason, the pilot of the soul; around this Being, and in this place dwells *true knowledge*. Here dwells divine reason, which is nourished by intelligence and *pure* knowledge ... Here reason finds its satisfaction, nourishment and joy in the vision of truth." [28]

Human souls see more or less of the eternal ideas, in proportion to the skill of the charioteer and the quality and discipline of the steeds. Those who, by fault of the charioteer or vice of the ignoble horse, are weighed down and fail of the vision limp away with broken wings and are nourished on *opinion*. For the ignoble horse, the appetitive power, by nature insatiable, is ever crying for more. It wants more pleasure, more wealth, more of all earthly things, and is thus ever pulling the chariot downward. The philosopher, being a good charioteer, succeeds in seeing much of the realm of truth.

According to Plato, while in company with the body, not even the process of "dying" which the philosopher practices—[29] i.e. detachment from the carnal and the material—can enable the soul to attain pure, unconfused knowledge. This is plainly stated in the *Phaedo*: "It has been proved to us by experience that if we would have pure knowledge of anything we must be quit of the body—the soul in herself must behold things in themselves; and then we shall attain the *wisdom* which we desire, and of which we say that we are *lovers*; not while we live, but *after death*. For if while in company with the body, the soul cannot have pure knowledge, one of two things follow—either knowledge is not to be attained at all, or, if at all, after death." [30] Thus, only after death is *pure* knowledge possible, and then only to the true philosopher.

This is very much in line with St. Paul's statement: "Now we see in a mirror, darkly; but then face to face: now I know in part; but then shall I know even as also I am known." [31]

I have spoken of eros; but what is eros? This question is best answered in *Symposium* 199c-212c. Eros is "something and desires something which it does not possess in itself." Eros then is aspiration. "Love is the love of *beauty* and wants and has not beauty." For Plato the beautiful is identical with the good. Eros then is the aspiration after the good apprehended as beauty. When a man desires the beautiful he desires the good and the happiness resulting from the possession of the good. All men, says Plato, desire to be happy; therefore all men are in love. But the word lover has incorrectly been restricted to those who feel sexual love.

Plato's view differs sharply from that of Freud, who regards sex as the only motive force of life, and aspiration after the ideas as merely a "sublimation" of the sexual impulse. For Plato as for Christianity love of the ideal is *sui generis*; it cannot be reduced to, or be explained in terms of, sexual love. Plato would have accused Freud of inverting the true order of things, of trying to explain the higher through the lower.

Plato's love differs also from Bergson's *élan vital*, the "vital impetus." The *élan vital* is purposeless, in the sense of not being directed to something ultimate; whereas Plato's love is directed towards the ideal. Like Bergson's *élan vital*, however, eros is *creative*. The sexual urge is the desire for physical immortality, for the achievement of a sort of endless existence in an infinite line of offspring.[32] Eros has also led the heroes in all ages to undergo dangers and even death for the sake of creating a name which shall be eternal.[33] Love spurs others to create works of the spirit. Such persons—philosophers, poets, other artists, and statesmen—create from the soul. And hence they attain a fairer immortality, for their creations are virtue, goodness, wisdom, and the laws that guide the State.[34]

The Platonic path of love passes from the concrete to the abstract, from the particular to the universal, from the personal to the impersonal. The true initiate rises from the love of bodies to the love of persons, then to the love of theories, next to that of institutions and communities, and finally to that of absolute, transcendent Beauty.

The contrast with Christian love is obvious. Christian love is, above all, love of the concrete personality; it is the love of every human person, and of a personal God. Christian love of man is founded on the recognition of the significance of each human soul, which is worth more than all the kingdoms of this world, being in the image of God. Plato's love, on the other hand, is, in its highest manifestations, love of the abstract, of the impersonal. Above love of the person he places love of theories, institutions and communities, and above these love of the Idea of Beauty.

For both Plato and Christianity the spiritual life is a life of love. For Christianity, indeed, love is the highest virtue. But for Plato love is purest, loftiest, when it aspires after abstract beauty, while for Christianity when it aspires after God, Who is a personal being.

But Santayana tells us[35] that love is "material," not spiritual, because it is based on a sense of want, a want of the beautiful, the good, and the perfect. He also tells us that spirit is *not* a respecter of *persons*. For Santayana personality is "poor, absurd, accidental." The true spiritual life for him is wholly disinterested, passive. He would, then, separate *noesis* and *eros*, keep the former but reject the latter; he would have intellect without aspiration. This is one of the most serious errors of contemporary philosophy. It is one of the chief causes of pragmatism. It has resulted also in Bergsonian intuitionism. The pragmatist, having separated the intellect from eros, places confidence in feeling, in will, and not in thought. Bergson divorces the intellect from eros and then says that the intellect cannot apprehend "duration." But Plato never claimed that intellect divorced from eros could apprehend reality. For him the philosopher searches for truth with his *whole* being. Bergson's criticism therefore applies to Santayana, but not to Plato. Abstract thought, the intellect alone, divorced from eros, leads to a false conception of reality. Likewise, eros divorced from intellection can only lead to a one-sided, impoverished philosophy.

We have seen that the soul has *three powers*: (1) the rational (*to logistikon*), (b) the spirited (*to thymoeides, thymos*), and (c) the appetitive (*to epithymetikon, epithymia*). The first of these consists of intellect and eros; the second, of conviction (*pistis*) and "spirit" (*thymos*); the third, of conjecture (*eikasia*) and desire (*epithymia*).[36] The rational power is wholly directed to the true, the good, and the beautiful; the spirited, to ruling, conquering, and getting fame;

the appetitive, to eating, drinking, other sensual pleasures, and material gain.

The rational and the appetitive faculties are opposed principles. The first fights against and restrains the second. In the struggle between reason and desire the spirited power usually sides with reason, and never takes part with desire against reason. Thus, when a man's desires violently prevail over his reason, the spirited principle is on the side of reason: the man is angry, reviles himself. Spirit stirs us to indignation when we see the just trampled under foot by the unjust. But if it is not controlled by reason it leads us to reckless boldness and self-assertion.

The proper exercise of each faculty is accompanied by a distinctive kind of pleasure. Plato distinguishes three kinds of pleasures. First, we have "material" pleasures, that is, pleasures that accompany the fulfillment of the desires of the appetitive faculty: the satisfaction of thirst, hunger, etc. Secondly, there is the pleasure of hope. A person is in an intermediate state when he is in actual suffering and yet remembers past pleasures, which, if they would only return, would relieve him. In such a case a man has both pleasure and pain. But when he is hungry or thirsty and has no hope of being filled he has double pain. Hopes are pictures conjured up with effort by the spirited power. The soul that has hope experiences pleasure:

it is joy we strive with when we have hope. Thirdly, there is the pleasure that accompanies the exercise of the rational faculty. This is the highest pleasure. Indeed, for Plato it is the only one that is genuine.

Another thing about the faculties of the human soul that should be noted is that each has its own distinctive governing element. The appetitive power is governed by conjecture (*eikasia*) which is based on memories of past experience. Conjecture governs expected pleasures and pains. Expected pleasures determine positive appetites, while expected pains determine aversion. The spirited power is governed by belief, conviction (*pistis*), which is based on tested experience. Such conviction broadly determines our hopes and fears. Lack of hope leads to despair; fears lead to indignation and shame. Belief is related to conjecture in the same way that tradition in the State is related to public opinion. The rational faculty is governed by *noesis*, by the apprehension of things independently of time, eidetically.

Plato founds his theory of virtue on his psychology. The faculties of the soul have distinct functions; the right performance of these functions produces mental well-being, inner health or virtue.

There are *four main virtues*: wisdom, courage, temperance, and justice. *Wisdom (sophia, phronesis)* is the virtue that pertains to the ra-

tional power. It consists in the knowledge of
what is for the true interest of each of the three
faculties of the soul, and in commanding and
counseling them in accordance with this knowledge. Thus wisdom is self-knowledge. It is
knowledge of what we are. And this means in
the first place the deep realization that each
of us is essentially not a body but a soul, which
is far superior to the body in worth and immortal. The wise man knows that the soul is the
real self and the body merely an instrument
of the soul. Some of us, remarks the Platonic
Socrates in *Alcibiades I*, confuse man himself
with his body, with the external tools he uses:
the eyes, hands, feet, and so on. But that which
is used is *different* from the *user*. The soul uses
the body that belongs to it, but is distinct from
the body and independent of it. Hence the man
who cherishes his body does *not* cherish *himself*,
but what *belongs* to him. He who tends money
tends neither himself nor his own things, and
is a stage further removed from himself. It is
the man who tends his *soul* who *really* tends
himself. Not what a man *has*, but what he *is*
constitutes his real dignity. Now when we have
a profound knowledge of what we are, then we
will know what is good for each part of our
nature and for our whole self.

Courage (andreia) pertains to the faculty that
comes next after the rational power in the hierarchical structure of the soul, namely, the spirited. This virtue consists in obedience of the

spirited power in pleasure and pain to the commands of reason.

Temperance (sophrosyne) belongs to all three parts of the soul, but specially to the third and lowest, the appetitive. It exists in the soul when the spirited and appetitive principles agree that the highest principle, reason, ought to rule and that they should obey. This virtue then consists in *proper subordination*, in the submission of the lower parts of the soul to the rule of the highest, without coercion.

Justice (dikaiosyne) is the *harmonious* working together of all three parts of the soul, where each does its own peculiar work and does not take over functions belonging to the other parts. Justice is a quality that results when wisdom, courage, and temperance are present; it is also a quality that preserves each of these. That is, it can be looked at both as an effect and as a cause.

Plato sometimes mentions *holiness (hosiotes)* as a fifth virtue. Holiness is rendering to the gods what is due to them: prayer and sacrifices.[37] In his later dialogues he tends to omit holiness as one of the virtues, probably because he came to think that properly it belonged to religion, not to philosophy.[38]

It is important to observe that while the virtues are distinct, they are not separate: they imply each other. An individual who possesses one virtue possesses all.

After defining the virtues in the *Republic*,

Plato remarks that it is evident that virtue is
the health, beauty, and well-being of the soul,
while vice is the disease, ugliness, and weakness
of the soul.[39] And he goes on to add that, this
being the case, it is ridiculous to ask which life
is preferable, the virtuous or the wicked, the
just or the unjust.

Let us now note again the hierarchical order
of the faculties of the human psyche. The rational principle, when wise, has care of the whole
psyche, it rules; and the spirited principle is
its subject and ally. Gymnastic strengthens the
spirited power, while music moderates and har-
monizes it with reason. Reason and the striving
power thus harmonized, and each perform-
ing its own function, will rule over the appetitive
principle and keep it confined to its own sphere
—they will not allow it to wax strong and en-
slave them. The rational and spirited principles
will thus be the best defenders of both soul and
body: reason counseling and the spirited element courageously executing reason's counsels
and commands.

3. Inversion of the Individual Life

There are, says Plato in the *Republic*, five
forms of State: the aristocratic, the timocratic,
the oligarchic, the democratic, and the tyrannic.
And there are five forms of individual life cor-
responding to these. Governments (*politeiai*), he
observes, vary as the characters (*ethe, tropoi*)

of men vary, and there must be as many kinds of the one as there are of the other. States grow out of human characters.[40]

We have already seen the *aristocratic* man: he is the virtuous individual, ruled by reason. It remains for us to consider the remaining four types of character. Let us begin with the *timocratic* or honor-loving man. He is a friend of the fine arts, but lacks understanding of them. He respects the hopes and fears of his ancestors; he has loyalty. But his guide is not wisdom, as for the aristocratic man, but law and custom. A man must be loyal to these, says Plato; but he must also be loyal to reason, and keep reason *above* law and custom. One must always see things in a *hierarchical* order. The error of the timocratic man lies in the fact that he fails to use his reason when he should. As a result he tends to confuse a particular version of the law with the law itself. So he rigorously obeys the letter of the law, often at the expense of its spirit. "He is somewhat self-willed and lacking in culture . . . , harsh to slaves . . . , gentle to the freeborn and very submissive to officials, a lover of office and of honor, a devotee of gymnastics and hunting . . . ; he is disdainful of wealth in his youth, but fond of it when he grows old." [41]

The timocratic man originates in a reaction against the character of his father: a brave man who dwells in an ill-governed city whose honors he declines, and who doesn't retaliate when

robbed. This reaction is encouraged by his
mother and by the old servants of the household.
The son becomes arrogant and ambitious,
whereas his aristocratic father was rational.

The *oligarchic* man is the son of the timocratic. He at first emulates his father, who is
perhaps a general or holds some other important
office. Then he sees his father dragged into
court by mischievous sycophants, put to death,
or banished, or outlawed, and losing all his
property. After seeing these things, and suffering
as a result of them, the son of the timocratic
man grows timid, dethrones the principle of
love of honor and enthrones the principle of
appetite and avarice, making it the great king
in his soul. He forces the rational and spirited
powers of the soul to act as the slaves of the
appetitive power. Reason now has "to calculate
and consider nothing but the ways of making
more money from a little, and the striving faculty to admire and honor nothing but riches and
rich men." [42]

The inversion is obvious. In the case of the
timocratic man, reason is subordinated to the
spirited principle, and the latter is made the
ruler of life. These two principles are now subordinated to the appetitive power. The culture
of the oligarchic man is but a thin gilding. His
virtue is an enforced virtue: he will cheat when
he can; he will be temperate in the satisfaction
of his bodily desires in order to be more intem-

perate in his accumulation of wealth; and he succeeds in keeping down his unnecessary desires only by force.

Let us now consider the origin of the *democratic* man. He is the son of the miserly oligarchic man, who has trained him in his own habits. Like his father, he keeps under by force his unnecessary desires. But gradually he is led away by wild associates and provided by them will all sorts of unnecessary pleasures, and ends up by not listening to fatherly counsel, the unnecessary desires having gained the upper hand. He calls "insolence 'good breeding,' license 'liberty,' prodigality 'magnificence,' and shamelessness 'manliness.' " [43] When his heyday is over, he readmits some of the exiled virtues and lives in a sort of equilibrium. But still he regards all pleasures alike. There is for him an equality of all desires, a failure to discriminate between the better and the worse. Moral standards have been discarded.

There is not even an inverted order in such an individual, as there is in the oligarchic man, but chaos. He has abandoned even the guidance of common opinion and conjecture by which the oligarchic man guides his life. He "lives out his life in this fashion, day by day indulging the appetite of the hour, now wine-bibbing and playing the flute, and again drinking only water and dieting; and at one time exercising his body, and sometimes idling and neglecting all things,

and at another time seeming to occupy himself
with philosophy. And frequently he goes in for
politics and bounces up and says and does whatever enters his head. And if military men excite
his emulation, thither he rushes, and if moneyed
men, to that direction he turns, and there is
no law or order in his existence; and he calls
this life of his the life of pleasure and freedom
and blessedness. . . . His life is motley and mani-
fold, and an epitome of the lives of many." [44]

A society which is made up of such individuals is finally destroyed by its main desire:
the inordinate craving for freedom. Too much
freedom breeds dissension and anarchy, and
finally the mob, under the leadership of a single
man, casts out its appointed rulers. Thus, out
of what Plato calls democracy, but which is
really *mobocracy*, there springs tyranny.

To tyranny there corresponds the *tyrannical*
man. How does he originate? He originates
out of the democratic man in precisely the same
way as the democratic man is formed out of
the oligarchic. The only difference is that the
tyrant goes to greater excesses and never re-
turns to any sort of equilibrium. He purges
out of himself every desire or opinion that is
deemed good, discards all self-control and
brings in madness to the full. He knows neither
respect for his parents nor friendship with anyone. He is made up of fierce base desires, which
he is ever feeding into greater size and number.

He lives a life farthest removed from reason.

If the oligarchic, the democratic, and the tyrannical man are all ruled by the lowest part of the soul, the appetitive, how can Plato distinguish them from one another? He does so by noting differences *within* the appetites of men. There are three types of appetites or desires: (a) the *necessary*, (b) the *un*necessary and *spendthrift*, and (c) the *lawless*. So there is a hierarchy within the appetitve power. The oligarchic man seeks to satisfy the *necessary* desires, and subjugates the other desires by force to these. But he goes too far in his efforts to provide for the gratification of the necessary desires. Thus, one needs material goods in order to live: one needs food, shelter and clothing. But the preoccupation of the oligarchic man with the provision for these needs becomes all-absorbing. Greed, miserliness, the worship of wealth constitute the distinguishing feature of such a man. The "democratic" man is ruled by the *un*necessary and spendthrift desires, while the tyrannical man is ruled by *lawless* desires, to which his other desires as well as reason and the spirited element are made subservient. Examples of lawless (*paranomoi*) desires cited by Plato are those for committing incest and murder. These desires are called unlawful, not only in the sense of being forbidden by human laws, but also by the higher principle of man, reason. The tyrannical man

has many unlawful desires, which are very
strong because his rational faculty as a moral
power is asleep, exercising no vigilance upon
them or disciplining them. One or several of
these desires become the ruling force in him,
the leader of his soul. It is nourished into greatness by his idle, spendthrift desires, until it
breaks out in frenzy. Such a man becomes "for
all his waking life the man he used to be from
time to time in his dreams, ready to shed blood
or do any dreadful deed." [45]

If such a man becomes a *public* tyrant, he
grows far more wicked and miserable than before, and reduces all the people to a slavery
of the harshest and bitterest form. Having been
nursed by the people into greatness, he stirs
up wars and impoverishes his subjects by the
imposition of heavy taxes. He gets rid of his
boldest followers, who joined in setting him up,
and purges the State of the wise and the brave.
Having impoverished the State by aggressive
wars, he feeds upon the people. They rebel,
and he beats them. "Thus excessive and un-
seasonable liberty passes into the harshest and
bitterest form of slavery." [46]

4. Knowledge, Freedom, and Responsibility

Plato, like Socrates, held that knowledge is
the strongest and most commanding thing. Yet
people are supposed to know the things that

are best for them and to act contrary to reason, because they are overcome by pain or pleasure. How is this to be reconciled with the view that reason is dominant? Plato takes up this problem in the *Protagoras*.[47] This popular view is for him erroneous. He shows that *on the popular* view pleasures are evil when they are followed by pain, and pains are good when they are followed by pleasure, but pleasure in itself is good and pain in itself is evil. To be overcome by pleasure is therefore to be overcome by the good. The good in such a case is unworthy only because there is less of it. To be overcome by pleasure therefore means to *choose less* good in place of greater good. Men are *not* overcome by *pleasure* to do something which though immediately pleasant will ultimately be painful, but rather by *ignorance*. They simply *misconceive* pain for pleasure. If a man thinks he is overcome by pleasure, knowing that the ultimate consequence will be pain, it is only because, as in vision, the nearer *seems* the greater thing. The many identify the good with the pleasant. They regard life as a process of selecting the greatest number of pleasures with the least amount of pain. But this *power to measure* pleasure and pain, good and evil, springs from *knowledge*, and the lack of power to measure correctly, or to be erroneously overpowered by pleasure, springs from the opposite of knowledge: *ignorance*. Ignorance is to have false opinion of, and be deceived in, matters where measuring is involved.

The discussion of this question brings to mind the role it has played in Western Christianity. In its treatment of the problem of evil, Christian theology in the West has at times viewed men as moral automata, some predestined to salvation and others to perdition. But such a view is against the very essence of true Christianity, which is a religion of freedom. Man for it is a free spiritual being. True Christianity is against fatalism and other kinds of determinism. It recognizes no favored group. All men have the capacity to become masters of themselves. Christianity agrees with Plato that man is not helpless in relation to pleasures and pains. It agrees with him that truth gives us real freedom: "You shall know the truth and the truth shall make you free." [48]

Although he recognizes and stresses freedom in truth, Plato does not dwell sufficiently on man's *initial* freedom, by which one may choose and cleave to truth and goodness, or may refuse to choose and cleave to them. His most striking affirmation of man's initial freedom appears in Book X of the *Republic*. "Virtue," says Plato, "is free, and as a man honors or dishonors her he will have more or less of her; the responsibility is with the chooser—God is blameless." [49] Christianity in its authentic form stresses both man's initial freedom, the freedom of choice, and his final freedom, the freedom in truth, in goodness.

Vastly different from both the Platonic and the Christian view is that so prevalent today, which makes man a completely helpless creature. This spirit is illustrated in the works of D. H. Lawrence, in which man appears as a function of sex. Psychoanalysis maintains the impotence of man to resist his desires and condemns their control as unhealthy "repression." This involves it in the glaring contradiction of at once denying and affirming the power of control in man. Men like Clarence Darrow do not hold the individual responsible for his acts. If a man is a liar or a criminal, something must have gone wrong with his thyroid or pituitary gland. We are being told by scientists that our conduct is determined by our chromosomes, glands, reflexes, and the like—by everything but ourselves, by our reason and will.

5. *General Inversion of Life*

The general inversion of life is illustrated by Plato's Myth of the Cave, in Book VII of the *Republic*.[50] In this myth Plato compares the mass of men to prisoners enchained from their childhood in a dark cavern. They have their backs to the entrance of the cavern and a fire is burning behind them, casting the shadows of the people that pass by, and of the objects they carry, on the wall of the den which the prisoners face. Chained, as far back as they can remember, so that they cannot walk or even turn their heads around, the *shadows seem to them to be the only realities.*

Now if one of these prisoners were released and turned around, he would be dazzled by the light and would not see the real objects. Hence he would persist in maintaining the sole truth of the shadows. When taken up to the light of the real world, he would not be able at first to see any realities but the shadows. Later, he would be able at night to see the stars and the moon. And finally he would be able to behold the sun. He would now pity his companions in the den. Upon returning there he would be unable at the beginning to see the shadows as distinctly as those persons who have never left it; and he would be ridiculed by the prisoners. They "would say that he had returned from his journey aloft with his eyes ruined and that it was not worth while even to attempt the ascent. And if it were possible to lay hands on and kill the man who tried to release them and lead them up, they would kill him." [51]

In this myth the life of the many is contrasted with the life of the true philosopher, the lover of true wisdom; the world of sense, with the world of the spirit; the transitory, with the eternal. The wisdom of the prisoners in the cave, which they value so much, is wisdom pertaining to phenomena. Their chains symbolize their attachment to this wisdom and to transitory material values. The great bulk of mankind is glued to the sense-world and considers happiness to consist in sensual pleasures and material possessions.

The journey upward is the ascent of the soul to the intelligible world, to the realm of the spirit, to that which is truly real. The philosopher ascends to that realm and then descends in order to enlighten those below. But sense-bound people ridicule him, refuse to accept his message and guidance to the realm of higher experience, thinking that they will leave behind the real world and enter the world of illusion.

Socrates is a brilliant example of those who have ascended, of those who have found reality and have despised the wisdom of "shadows." He discovered the real world in and through man. Hence his stress on self-knowledge. Natural science, which advances in the realm of "shadows," of the senses, will never solve the riddle of the universe. This riddle can only be solved by penetration into man's moral and religious experience. Being can only be known through man. Such a view is essentially Christian. The Founder of Christianity remarked: "The kingdom of God cometh not with observation: neither shall they say, Lo here! or, lo there! for, behold, the kingdom of God is within you." [52]

It is very sad to observe that most modern

philosophers have failed to take cognizance of
this profound truth. They have made the Cave,
the realm of quantity and of the senses, their
permanent abode. "Nearly all our philosophers," as Hans Driesch points out, "carefully
eschew, and pretend not to see the problem
of immortality, and certain formalistic philosophers only admit 'significant' problems within the framework of mathematics." [53] Logical
positivists consider such problems as those of
the destiny of man, his relations to God, the
nature of good and evil, as "meaningless." Anything that cannot be verified by sense-experience, they tell us, is meaningless; and hence
it is ridiculous to ask such questions. The realm
of the spirit is a fiction, only the realm of the
senses is real. Hence they concern themselves
with phenomena alone, with the ephemeral and
not with the eternal.

Other philosophers have started with a state
of doubt as regards the reality of the realm
beyond that of the senses, and never overcame
their doubt. They spend their entire life dealing
with epistemological questions, investigating
and reinvestigating the capacities of the mind
for knowledge, ever getting ready to ascend
from the Cave to the supersensible, but never
making the ascent, never getting to metaphysics. They restrict themselves to the study of
knowledge and fail to get to being.

According to Socrates and Plato, the man

who has knowledge of the self knows where
reality is. But today, more than ever before,
man is ignorant of himself. Our life is inverted.
We no longer cherish our true self. We are en-
slaved to material things. Ours is a life of the
senses, not of reason and love. Our age is one
in which spiritual aspirations have been pushed
aside and bodily interests have taken control.

The life of modern man is dominated not
by religion or spiritually oriented philosophy,
but by the sciences of inert matter: by me-
chanics, physics, chemistry, and so on. The subjects that engross our attention are not religious
or ethical. We spend our time laboring and con-
suming, scattering our energies in the satisfaction of unnecessary desires and in the distractions created by industrial, technological, ma-
terialistic civilization.

It is within our power to transform our lives,
to restore the proper order within ourselves,
giving primacy to spiritual over material values.
No task is more urgent, no work more glorious
than the regeneration of individuals and of
states. In the *Euthyphro* Plato calls it "the most
beautiful work" (*pankalon ergon*), which man
can accomplish with divine aid.[54]

SELECTED PASSAGES FROM PLATO'S DIALOGUES ON MAN AND THE HUMAN SOUL*

I. NATURE OF MAN

1. Man Is a Soul Using a Body

(*Note:* Plato holds that man is really the soul, not the body, or the soul together with the body. Man is a soul using a body as an instrument. Plato's conception of man obviously differs here from the Christian, according to which man is the composite of soul and body. However, Christianity is close to Plato in holding that *principally* man is not the body but the soul. In *Alcibiades I*, his argument for this view proceeds as follows.)

Socrates. Could we ever know what art makes a man better, if we did not know what we ourselves are?

* Translated by C. Cavarnos.

Alcibiades. Impossible.

Soc. Now is it an easy thing to know oneself (*gnonai heauton*), and was it an ordinary man who inscribed these words on the temple at Delphi? Or is it a difficult thing to know oneself, and not something to be achieved by anybody?

Alc. It has often seemed to me, Socrates, that self-knowledge can be achieved by anybody; but at other times, that it is very difficult.

Soc. But whether it is easy or not, Alcibiades, the matter for us stands thus: if we have this knowledge, we shall be likely to take care of ourselves, but if we are ignorant, we never can.

Alc. That is true.

Soc. Well, then, in what way can what possesses self-identity be discovered? For in this way we are likely to discover what we are ourselves; but so long as we are ignorant of it, we cannot.

Alc. That is so.

Soc. Come, now, I beseech you, tell me with whom are you talking now? Is it not with me?

Alc. Yes.

Soc. And I with you?

Alc. Yes.

Soc. Socrates, then, is the one who is talking?

Alc. No doubt.

Soc. And Alcibiades is the one who is hearing?

Alc. Yes.

Soc. And in talking Socrates uses speech?

Alc. Certainly.

Soc. And you call, I suppose, talking and using speech the same thing?

Alc. To be sure.

Soc. Now is not the user different from the thing which he uses?

Alc. How do you mean?

Soc. For example, a shoemaker uses a square tool, a circular tool, and others for cutting.

Alc. Yes.

Soc. But the cutter and user is different from the tools which he uses in cutting?

Alc. Of course.

Soc. And in the same way the instrument of the harper is different from the harper himself?

Alc. Yes.

Soc. Now the question which I just asked was whether you think that the user is always different from what he uses.

Alc. I do.

Soc. Then what shall we say of the shoemaker? Does he cut with his tools only, or with his hands also?

Alc. With his hands also.

Soc. So he uses these too?

Alc. Yes.

Soc. Does he use his eyes, too, in shoemaking?

Alc. Yes.

Soc. And we admit that the user is different from the things which he uses?

Alc. Yes.

Soc. Hence the shoemaker and the harper are different from the hands and eyes which they use?

Alc. Evidently.

Soc. And does not a man use his whole body?

Alc. Certainly.

Soc. And that which uses is different from that which is used?

Alc. Yes.

Soc. Hence man is different from his own body (*soma*)?

Alc. It seems so.

Soc. What, then, is man?

Alc. I cannot say.

Soc. But you can say that he is that which uses the body.

Alc. Yes.

Soc. Now is there anything else that uses the body but the soul (*psyche*)?

Alc. Nothing else.

Soc. The soul, then, rules it?

Alc. Yes.

Soc. Now I think no one will dissent from the following assertion.

Alc. What is it?

Soc. That man is one of three things.

Alc. What things?

Soc. Soul, body, or both together constituting a whole.

Alc. Very well.

Soc. But did we not admit that what actually

rules the body is man?

Alc. We did.

Soc. Now does the body rule over itself?

Alc. By no means.

Soc. For we said that it is ruled.

Alc. Yes.

Soc. Surely then this cannot be what we are seeking.

Alc. It seems not.

Soc. Then does the combination of the two rule over the body, and hence this is man?

Alc. Perhaps.

Soc. This is the least likely of all things; for if one of the members does not share in the rule, the combination of the two cannot possibly be ruling.

Alc. Right.

Soc. But since neither the body, nor the combination of the body and the soul is man, it follows, I suppose, that either man is nothing, or if he is something, it turns out that he is nothing else than soul.

Alc. Just so.

Soc. Is anything clearer required to prove to you that the soul is man?

Alc. Certainly not; I think this has been adequately proved.

Soc. And if it has been proved sufficiently, though not precisely, we are satisfied. We shall attain exact knowledge when we have discovered that which we passed over just now, because it would involve much reflection.

Alc. What was that?

Soc. That which was said a little while ago, that we must first consider what possesses self-identity; but now, instead of what possesses self-identity we have considered the nature of particular beings. And perhaps this will suffice; for surely there is nothing which we may more properly call ourselves than the soul.

Alc. No, indeed.

Soc. Then we may rightly think thus, that you and I are conversing with one another, using words, soul to soul.

Alc. Quite so.

Soc. Well, that is just what we were saying a little earlier—that Socrates is conversing with Alcibiades, using words, talking not with your face, as it seems, but with the real Alcibiades, that is, with his soul.

Alc. I think so.

Soc. Hence, he who enjoins self-knowledge bids us to gain knowledge of the soul.

Alc. So it seems.[1]

* * *

(*Note*: That the real self is not the body but the soul is emphasized also in the *Phaedo*. Socrates, having been condemned to death by the Athenians on false charges, is about to die in prison by drinking hemlock. One of Socrates' friends, Crito, asks him for final instructions

about his children and other matters, particular-
ly his burial. Socrates uses Crito's question as
an occasion to stress the view that the real
self of a man is not his body, and hence burial
is *not* the burial of a *man* but of a man's *body*.)

When he had finished speaking, Crito said:
"Well, Socrates, do you have any commands
for us, either about your children or about anything else in which we can serve you?"

"What I always tell you, Crito," he replied,
"nothing new. If you take care of yourselves,
you will be rendering a service to me and mine
and to yourselves, whatever you do, even if
you do not promise now to do so. But if you
neglect yourselves and do not desire to live
in the manner which I have indicated just now
and on previous occasions, even if at present
you make many and strong promises, you will
accomplish nothing."

"Well, we will exert ourselves to do that,"
he replied. "But in what way shall we bury
you?"

"In whatever way you wish," he said, "if
you can get hold of me and I do not run away
from you. And he smiled, and gazing steadfastly
at us he said: I cannot persuade Crito, my
friends, that I am the same Socrates who is
now conversing and ordering each part of the
argument; he thinks that I am the other Socrates, whom he will later see a dead body, and
he asks how he will bury me. And though I

have said just now a great deal indicating that
after I drink the poison I shall no longer remain
with you, but will go away to the joys of the
blessed, he seems to think that I mean something
else, that I am merely conforting you and myself. Therefore," he said, "be surety for me
to Crito . . . that I shall not remain when I die,
but shall go away, in order that he may bear
my death more easily, and not be grieved when
he sees my body being burned or buried, as
if *I* were undergoing tribulations, or say at the
burial that he is laying out Socrates, or is following him to the grave, or is burying him. Realize,
excellent Crito, that not speaking rightly is not
only an offense, but also infects the soul with
evil. You must be of good courage then and
say that you are burying my *body*." [2]

* * *

(*Note:* In the *Laws*, which was written much
later than the *Phaedo*, Plato again identifies
man with the soul. And as in the preceding
passage, he remarks that at death it is not
man that dies and is buried, but his body.)

The soul is altogether superior to the body,
and in actual life it is the soul and nothing else
that makes each one of us to be what he is,
while the body is a likeness that accompanies
each of us. When we are dead, our bodies are
well said to be images of the dead; for the real
self of each one of us, which is called the im-

mortal soul, goes away to other gods, to give
an account to them (as the law of our fathers
says)—a thing with regard to which the virtuous
are of good cheer, while the bad are very fearful.
No great help can be given to the departed one.
It was when he lived that all his kindred should
have helped him, so that during his life he may
have been as just and holy as possible, and that
after death, in the life that follows this, he may
be free from punishment for badness and sins.
This being so, one should not spend wastefully
on the dead, thinking that the mass of flesh
which is being buried is eminently his own rela-
tive. He should consider that his son, or brother,
or whoever else it may be that he thinks he
is burying with grief, has departed to complete
and fulfill his own destiny.[3]

2. Man Is a Heavenly Creature

We are not an earthly but a heavenly plant
(*phyton ouk engeion all' ouranion*).[4]

3. Man Alone of All Living Creatures
Has a Sense of Rhythm and Harmony

Whereas all other living creatures are devoid
of perception of the order and disorder in move-
ments, which we term rhythm and harmony,
to us men the gods have given the pleasurable
perception of rhythm and harmony.[5]

4. *Man Is the Most Religious of All Living Creatures*

Man is the most God-revering (*theosebestaton*) of all living creatures.[6]

5. *Man Is Potentially God-like*

God is in no way unrighteous, but is perfectly righteous; and there is nothing so like Him as one of us who is the most righteous.[7]

II. NATURE OF THE SOUL

1. *The Soul Is Dynamic, Self-active*

Athenian. What is the definition of that which has for its name soul? Have we any other than that which has already been given: the motion (*kinesis*) which is able to move itself?

Cleinias. Are you asserting that the very same substance (*ousia*) which is named by all of us "soul" has as its definition "that which is self-moved"?

Athenian. That is what I am asserting.[8]

* * *

He who asserts that self-motion is the essence and the very definition of the soul will not be put to shame. For every body that derives its motion from without is soulless, but that which

is moved from within has a soul. Now if this
is so—that that which is self-moving is nothing
else than the soul—then the soul must of necessity be immortal.[9]

2. *"Motions" or Activities of the Soul*

(*Note*: The "motions" or activities of the
soul are many and diverse. They are not only
thoughts, judgments, and beliefs, but also vo-
litions, emotions, and desires.)

The motions of the soul are named wish, contemplation, care, deliberation, opinion true and
false, joy, sorrow, confidence, fear, hate, love
and so on.[10]

* * *

Socrates. The soul has a certain work which
nothing else can perform—I mean such actions
(*praxeis*) as to take care, to exercise control,
to deliberate and the like. Can these be rightly
assigned to anything other than the soul, as her
proper actions?

Thrasymachus. To nothing else.[11]

* * *

Socrates. Do you not regard anger, fear,
longing, sorrow, love, zeal, envy and the like
as feelings that belong to the soul only?

Protarchus. I do.[12]

* * *

Socrates. Do you mean by thinking (*dianoei-sthai*) what I mean?

Theaetetus. What do you mean?

Soc. I mean the conversation which the soul holds with herself about whatever she is considering. . . . The soul when thinking seems to me to be doing nothing else than conversing with herself, asking questions and answering them, affirming and denying. . . . What do *you* mean by thinking?

Theaet. The same.[13]

* * *

Stranger. Thought and speech are the same, except that the former, which is the unuttered dialogue of the soul with herself, has been named thought.

Theaetetus. Quite true.

Str. But the stream which flows from the soul through the mouth and is audible has been called speech.

Theaet. True.

Str. And we know that in speech there is—

Theaet. What?

Str. Affirmation and negation.

Theaet. Yes, we know it.

Str. When the affirmation or negation in the soul takes place mentally only, in silence, have you any other name for it but opinion?

Theaet. Certainly not.[14]

* * *

(*Note*: The apprehension or perception of universals, unlike that of sense-objects, such as particular colors and sounds, is regarded by Plato as an activity of the soul that is not mediated by bodily organs.)

Socrates. The soul views (*episkopei*) some things by herself directly, and others through the faculties of the body.[15] That is my opinion. What do you think?

Theaetetus. I am of the same opinion.

Soc. Now to which class do you assign being? for this most certainly is an attribute of all things.

Theaet. I assign it to the class which the soul apprehends by herself directly.

Soc. Would you say this also of similarity and dissimilarity, sameness and otherness?

Theaet. Yes.

Soc. How about the beautiful and the ugly, good and evil?

Theaet. It seems to me that these are among those objects whose essence the soul views in relation to one another, reflecting within herself things past and present in relation to those of the future.[16]

3. *Soul Is the Source of Life in the Body*

Socrates. Tell me, what is that of which the inherence in the body renders the body alive?

Cebes. The soul.

Soc. Now is this always the case?

Cebes. Yes, of course.

Soc. Therefore, whatever the soul takes possession of to that she always brings life (*zoe*)?

Cebes. Certainly.[17]

* * *

Those who gave the soul her name (*psyche*) intended to express this, that when the soul is present in the body she is the cause of its being alive, giving it the power to breathe and reviving it, and when this reviving power fails the body perishes and dies.[18]

4. *Soul Rules the Body*

When the soul and the body are united, nature orders the body to serve and be ruled, and the soul to rule and be master.[19]

* * *

"Well," said Socrates, "in your opinion, is there anything other than the soul—especially the wise soul—that rules all parts of man?

"Indeed, no," replied Simmias.

"And does the soul yield to the passions of the body or does she oppose them? For example, when the body is hot and thirsty, does not the soul incline us against drinking? and when the body is hungry, against eating? And in a myriad of other instances do we not see the soul opposing the body?"

"No doubt."

"Now did we not agree earlier that if the soul were a harmony [i.e. a by-product of the body], she could never utter a note at variance with the tensions, relaxations, vibrations and other changes of the elements of which it is composed, that she could only follow and never lead them?"

"Yes," he replied, "we agreed."

"Well then, is she not found now by us to be acting in exactly the opposite way, leading all those elements of which someone [the materialist] says she is composed, and in almost everything opposing them throughout life, and coercing them in every way, sometimes chastening the body more harshly and painfully by means of gymnastic and medicine, and sometimes more gently, now threatening and now admonishing, talking to the desires, propensities

and fears, as being something distinct from
them . . . ?"

"Yes, Socrates, I certainly think so." [20]

* * *

It would be a most true statement, then, to
say that according to the natural order (*kata
physin*) the soul rules and the body is ruled.[21]

5. *Soul Is the Seat of the Virtues*

(*Note*: The intellectual and moral excel-
lences or virtues—wisdom, courage, temperance, justice, etc.—are qualities that belong not
to the body but to the soul. They are perfections
of the soul which render her beautiful.)

Socrates. If the soul, my dear Alcibiades, is
to know herself, she must look at a soul, and
above all at that part of her in which resides
the virtue (*arete*) of wisdom and at any other
part of the soul that is like it?

Alcibiades. I think so, Socrates.

Soc. Now is there any part of the soul that
is more divine than this, which is the seat of
knowledge and wisdom?

Alc. There is none.[22]

* * *

A man should be confident about his soul,

if in his life he has renounced the pleasures
and ornaments of the body, considering them
alien to him and working harm rather than good,
and has eagerly sought the pleasures of learning
and has adorned his soul not with alien ornaments, but with her own proper ones: temperance, justice, courage, freedom, and truth.[23]

* * *

Virtue is the health and beauty and vigor
of the soul, while vice is the disease and ugliness
and weakness of the soul.[24]

6. Soul Is Akin to the Divine

The soul is akin to the divine (*theion*) and
immortal and eternal.[25]

* * *

When the soul investigates alone [without
the use of the body], she departs into the realm
beyond, the region of the pure, the eternal, the
immortal, the unchangeable, and being akin to
these, she always dwells with them whenever
she is by herself and is not hindered; and she
has rest from her wanderings, and does not
change, because she is in contact with the unchanging.[26]

* * *

Of all the things which belong to a man, his soul is the most divine.[27]

7. *Care of the Soul*

I[28] do nothing but go about persuading you, old and young, to care (*epimeleisthai*) neither for your bodies nor for money more than for the perfection of your souls, or even as much. I tell you that virtue does not come from money, but from virtue comes money and every other good of man, both private and public.[29]

* * *

In truth, there neither is nor will there ever be anything of greater importance than the cultivation (*paideusis*) of the soul.[30]

* * *

Since the soul is seen to be immortal, she cannot escape from evils or attain salvation in any other way than by becoming as good and wise as possible. For the soul takes nothing with her to the other world but her education and her character, and these are said to benefit or injure the departed greatly from the very beginning of his journey there.[31]

* * *

You must not attempt to cure the eyes without the head, or the head without the . . . soul. For all that is good and all that is bad in the

body and in the whole man originates in the soul,
and flows from there, as from the head into
the eyes. Therefore, it is necessary to treat the
soul first and foremost, if the head and the rest
of the body are to be well. Now the treatment
of the soul is by means of certain *epodai*—
good and beautiful discourses. Through these,
temperance is engendered in our souls, and
when it is engendered and present, it is easy
to secure health to the head and the rest of
the body.[32]

* * *

When a man is healthy and temperate, and
before he goes to sleep awakens his rational
faculty and feeds it on noble discourses and
thoughts, and enters a state of meditation (*syn-
noia*); and has exercised moderation with respect to the wants of the appetitive power, so
that it may sleep and not trouble the highest
faculty through its pleasures and pains, but
leave it by itself, alone, pure to aspire after,
apprehend and contemplate what it did not
know, things either past, present or future; and
likewise has calmed the spirited element, so that
he may not fall asleep with his anger excited
against any one—when, I say, he has quieted
the two irrational powers of the soul and aroused
the third power, which is the seat of wisdom,
then especially he attains truth and it is least

likely that he will have unlawful visions in his dreams.[33]

* * *

We must take care that a teacher of doctrines (*mathemata*), which are food for the soul, does not deceive us, like the merchant and the retail-dealer, who sell food for the body. For the latter praise all their goods, although neither they know what is good and what is bad for the body, nor those who buy from them, unless one happens to be a trainer or physician. In the same manner, those who take their doctrines about in cities and sell them by retail to the person who desires them, praise everything that they sell, although, my excellent friend, probably some of them are ignorant which of their wares is good and which is bad for the soul; and their customers are similarly ignorant, unless one happens to be a physician of the soul. If then you happen to possess knowledge as to which of these is good and which is bad, it will be safe for you to buy doctrines from Protagoras or from anyone else; but if not, my friend, watch lest you hazard what is dearest to you on the toss of the dice. For indeed there is far greater peril in the purchase of doctrines than in the purchase of eatables. For when you buy eatables and drinks from the retail-dealer or the merchant, it is possible to carry them off in other vessels, and before you receive them into the body by eating or drinking them it is possible to lay them down at your home and call in a person who has knowledge about such things, and get his advice as to which is good to eat or drink and which is not, and how much, and when; hence the peril in this purchase is not great. In the case of doctrines, however, it is not possible to take them away in another vessel, but having paid for them, you must receive the doctrines into your very soul, and go away either harmed or benefited.[34]

* * *

Men ought to honor (*timan*) their own souls. But there is hardly anyone of us who honors the soul rightly, although we think we do. . . . He who thinks that he can magnify his soul by certain words or gifts, or by certain compliances, while he is not making her at all better, fancies that he is honoring her; but he does not really do so. . . . Again, when a man does not regard himself responsible for his own sinful acts and for many and great evils, which he has committed from time to time, and always exempts himself from blame, he thinks he is honoring his soul; but he is far from doing so, for he actually is injuring her. . . . Again, when a man prefers bodily beauty to virtue, this is nothing else than a real and total dishonor of the soul. For such preference implies that the body is more honorable than the soul,—falsely, since nothing earth-

born is more honorable than the heavenly. . . .
And again, when a man desires to acquire money
in a dishonest manner, or feels no qualms in
thus acquiring money, he does not then by his
gifts honor his soul. He fails altogether to do
this, for he barters away her glory and beauty
for a piece of gold; yet all the gold on the earth
and under it is not worth as much as virtue. . .

Speaking generally, honoring the soul consists in following what is better and in improv-
ing, as far as we can, what is inferior, when
this is susceptible of improvement. And man
has no possession that is by nature more fitted
than the soul for avoiding evil and tracking out
and taking what is best, and living in fellowship
with it, when he has espoused it, for the remain-
der of his life.[35]

NOTES

THE PROBLEM OF THE DESTINY OF MAN

1. V. 475d.
2. *Theaet.* 174b; cf. *Alc.* I. 129b.
3. Cf. *Rep.* II. 379c; *Laws* X. 906a; *Epin.* 973c, 974a.
4. *Rep.* X. 604c.
5. *Phaedo* 118; cf. *Seventh Epistle* 324e.
6. Cf. *Rep.* VIII. 546a ff.
7. The words are Shakespeare's (*Macbeth*, Act V, Scene 4), but the thought is to be found also in Plato's Myth of the Cave, *Rep.* VII.
8. *Phaedo* 91d.
9. This is the cry of Chatoff in Dostoievsky's novel *The Demons*.
10. Cf. *Meno* 18b; *Laches* 186a; *Phaedo* 107c.
11. Cf. for example the arguments in the *Phaedo*.
12. *Apol.* 35a; cf. *Cleit.* 408a.
13. *Rep.* X. 618c; *Laws* VII. 803b.
14. 526d-e; cf. 487e-488a.
15. *Alc.* I. 129b.
16. *Ibid.*
17. *Rep.* VI-VII; *Seventh Epistle* 344b; cf. *Phaedr.* 270c.
18. *Tim.* 28c; *Seventh Epistle* 341c-e.

19. *Phaedo* 78a; *Tim.* 21e-25d; *Laws* II. 657ff.

20. 987e. About the authorship of the *Epinomis* see W. Jaeger, *Paideia*, Vol. III, p. 214.

21. 344d, 341c-d.

22. Cf. especially *Tim.*, *Phil.*, *Laws* X, *passim*.

23. For the immanence of God see *Tim.*, *Stat.*, and *Laws* X, *passim;* for God's transcendence see *Tim.* 42e and *Stat.* 272e.

24. *Tim.* 28c, 37c, 41a; *Phil.* 28c; *Laws* X. 903d, 904a.

25. *Rep.* II, 379b-c, 380a, III. 391c; *Tim.* 30a; *Laws* X. 896e ff.

26. *Laws* X. 903b.

27. *Tim.* 41a-b.

28. *Laws* X. 903d.

29. *Rep.* VI. 501b; *Tim.* 90a.

30. *Tim.* 90b-c.

31. *Theaet.* 176b.

32. *Laws* IV. 716b.

33. *Rep.* VI. 500c.

34. *Phil.* 51c-d, 64e.

35. *Tim.* 90d. Cf. *Laws* VII. 818c-d.

36. *Rep.* VI. 500c-d.

37. *Soph.* 228ff.; cf. *Alc. I* 117c-118a, *Laws* IX. 863c.

38. *Soph.* 229c; *Phil.* 48e.

39. *Phil.* 49a.

40. *Soph.* 230d.

41. *Ibid.* 231e.

42. *Rep.* VI. 511b.

43. *Ibid.* VII. 540a.

44. *Ibid.* VI. 508e.

45. *Ibid.* VII. 518c-d; *Symp.* 210-212a.

46. *Symp.* 212a.

47. *Tim.* 42e; cf. *Stat.* 272e.

48. *Rep.* VII. 519c ff., 540b.

THE INDIVIDUAL LIFE

1. In the original version of my essay, there is no reference to the English publication from which these statements were taken; and I cannot now recall where I found them, thirty-three years having elapsed since then. Recently, while reading the first volume of Boris Brasol's translation of *The Diary of a Writer* (London, 1949), I found these statements of Dostoievsky, worded somewhat differently, on pp. 540, 541, 542.

2. Solovyev, *God, Man, and the Church*, London, 1937, p. 21.

3. 206-212.

4. IV. 713e.

5. *Letters and Social Aims*, rev. ed., Boston, 1894, pp. 313-317.

6. *Through Nature to God*, Boston and New York. 1899, pp. 188-190.

7. *Creative Evolution*, London, 1913, p. 283.

8. *Rep.* X. 608d-611a.

9. *Phaedo* 70c-72d.

10. *Ibid.* 113e-114c. In the *Apology* (403-41c) Socrates views the souls in the beyond as retaining their personal traits.

11. *Ibid.* 72e-77d, 91e-92a.

12. *Ibid.* 78b-84b.

13. See e.g. *Introduction to Metaphysics*, New York and London, 1912, pp. 38-39.

14. *Phaedo* 79a-80b.

15. *Ibid.* 100b-107b.

16. *Phaedr.* 245c-246a; *Laws* X. 893b-896d.

17. *Phaedo* 80a-e; *Rep.* VI. 501b; *Tim.* 41a-b, 90a.

18. *Critique of Practical Reason*.

19. *Outlines of Psychology*.

20. *The Eternal Life*.

21. *Tim.* 41a-b.

22. *Outlines of Psychology*, Boston, 1886, p. 118.

23. *Gorg.* 523a-b; *Rep.* X. 615a-c.

24. *Phaedo* 107c-d.

25. Cf. *Rep.* II. 361e-362a, X. 614a.

26. 246-257.

27. R. Demos, ed., *The Dialogues of Plato*, Vol. I, New York, 1937, p. xi.

28. *Phaedr.* 247c-d.

29. *Phaedo* 67.

30. *Ibid.* 66e-67a.

31. 1 Cor. 13:12.

32. *Symp.* 208e; *Laws* IV. 721c.

33. *Symp.* 208c-e.

34. *Ibid.* 209a-e.

35. George Santayana, *Platonism and the Spiritual Life.*

36. *Rep.* IV. 435-442, V. 580-1.

37. Cf. *Euthyphro* 14.

38. Cf. *Rep.* IV. 427b-c.

39. *Ibid.* 444d-e.

40. *Ibid.* 445c, V. 544d.

41. *Rep.* VIII. 548e-549b.

42. *Ibid.* 553c-d.

43. *Ibid.* 560e-561a.

44. *Ibid.* 561c-e.

45. *Rep.* IX. 574e.

46. *Rep.* VIII. 569c.

47. 352b ff.

48. John 8:32.

49. 617e.

50. *Rep.* VII. 514a ff.

51. *Ibid.* 517a.

52. Luke 17:20-21.

53. Driesch, *Psychical Research: The Science of the Supernormal*, London, 1933, p. 160.

54. 13e, 14b.

SELECTED PASSAGES FROM PLATO'S
DIALOGUES ON MAN AND THE HUMAN SOUL

1. *Alcibiades* I 128e-131a.
2. *Phaedo* 115a-e.
3. *Laws* XII. 959a-c.
4. *Tim.* 90a; cf. *Rep.* VI. 500b.
5. *Laws* II. 653e; cf. 664e-665a.
6. *Laws* X. 902b; *Tim.* 41e-42a; *Menex.* 237d-e.
7. *Theaet.* 176c; cf. *Rep.* VI. 501b.
8. *Laws* X. 895e-896a.
9. *Phaedr.* 245e-246a.
10. *Laws* X. 896e-897a.
11. *Rep.* I. 353d.
12. *Phil.* 47e.
13. *Theaet.* 189e-190a.
14. *Soph.* 263e-264a.
15. The senses of sight, hearing, and so on.
16. *Theaet.* 185e-186b.
17. *Phaedo* 105c-d.
18. *Crat.* 399d-e.
19. *Phaedo* 79e-80a.
20. *Ibid.* 94b-95a.
21. *Laws* X. 896b-c.
22. *Alc.* I. 133b-c.
23. *Phaedo* 114d-115a.
24. *Rep.* IV. 444d-e.
25. *Rep.* X. 611e.
26. *Phaedo* 79c-d.
27. *Laws* V. 726; cf. 728b.
28. Socrates.
29. *Apol.* 30a-b.
30. *Phaedr.* 241c; cf. *Laws* V. 727a.
31. *Phaedo* 107c-d.

32. *Charm.* 156c-157a.
33. *Rep.* IX. 571d-572b.
34. *Prot.* 313c-314b.
35. *Laws* V. 727a-728d.

INDEX

INDEX